**This book is to be returned on or before
the last date stamped below.**

Ant

Written by Stephen Savage

Illustrated by Clive Pritchard

Wayland

OBSERVING NATURE

Ant	Blackbird
Duck	Frog
Butterfly	Oak tree
Rabbit	Seagull

.si

y

d

e

gland

blishers) Ltd

Publication Data

n

Ant. - (Observing Nature Series)
I. Title II. Pritchard, Clive III. Series
595.796

ISBN 0-7502-1287-X

Typeset by Jean Wheeler
Printed and bound in Italy by
G. Canale & C.S.p.A., Turin
Typeset by Jean Wheeler

OBSERVING NATURE

Ant

Written by Stephen Savage

Illustrated by Clive Pritchard

Wayland

OBSERVING NATURE

Ant	Blackbird
Duck	Frog
Butterfly	Oak tree
Rabbit	Seagull

Series editor: Francesca Motisi
Designer: Jean Wheeler

First published in 1995 by
Wayland (Publishers) Ltd
61 Western Road, Hove
East Sussex BN3 1JD, England

British Library Cataloguing in Publication Data
Savage, Stephen
Ant. - (Observing Nature Series)
I. Title II. Pritchard, Clive III. Series
595.796

ISBN 0-7502-1287-X

Typeset by Jean Wheeler
Printed and bound in Italy by
G. Canale & C.S.p.A., Turin
Typeset by Jean Wheeler

Contents

What is an ant?

There are several different types of ant, but the

black ant is the type most people see.

Like most ants, they live

underground in

a large nest.

Ants are a type of insect. They have a large head, two big eyes and long antennae. The body has two parts, a small middle part and a large abdomen at the end. As you will see later, some black ants have wings.

The female

The ant colony is made up of three different types of ant, the queen, the males and the workers. All worker ants are females. They do not have wings and cannot lay eggs.

It is the worker ant that we normally see.

These ants look after the nest and find food.

The worker ants have poor eyesight but they

use their antennae for taste, touch and smell.

The male

The male ants have wings and
are slightly larger than the workers.
Male ants are not found in the nest
all year round. They hatch only
in the summer when they
will be ready for
the mating
flight.

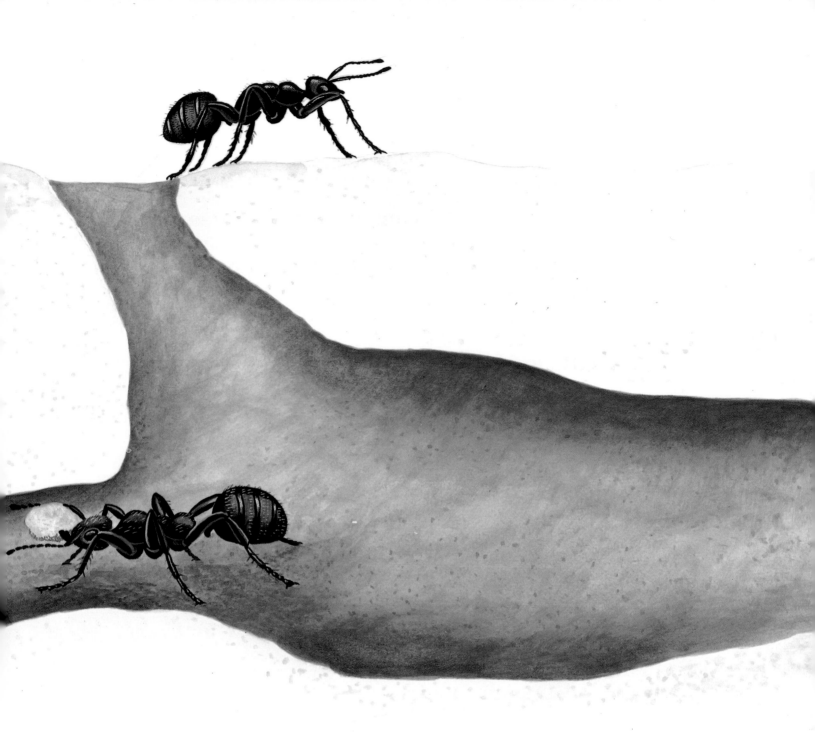

The males do not have to gather food or feed themselves.
They stay hidden in the nest and are looked after by the
worker ants.

The queen

Life in the ant nest is centred around the queen and her eggs. Out of all the thousands of ants, she is the only one that can lay eggs. Most of the eggs will become worker ants, some male ants and a few will be new queens.

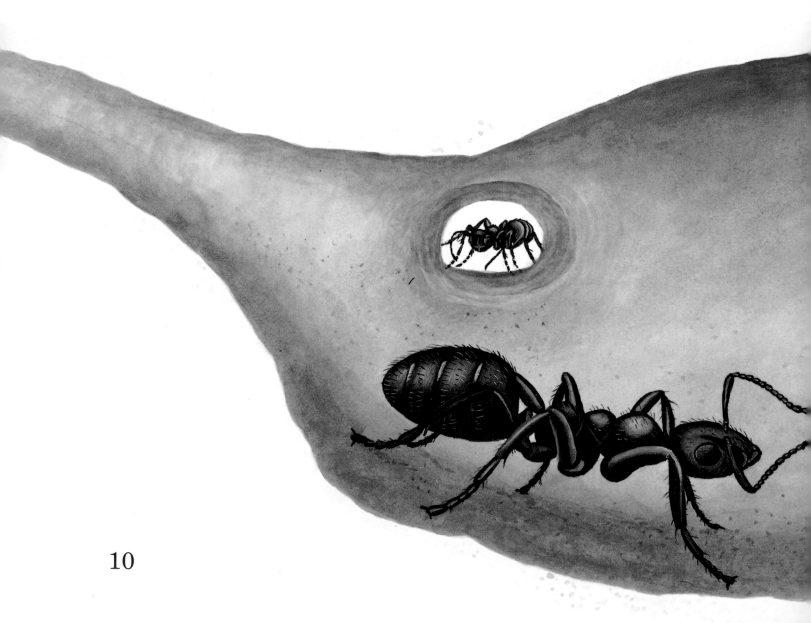

A queen ant has wings when she first hatches but gets rid of them after she has mated. Then she is ready to start a new colony.

Looking for food

Some of the worker ants search for food. They leave
scent trails on the ground so that they can find their
way back to the nest. When a worker ant finds a large
amount of food, it returns to the nest for help.

The food is carried in the ant's strong jaws. You can often see worker ants travelling to and from the nest following the scent trails. Ants often eat other insects and food crumbs.

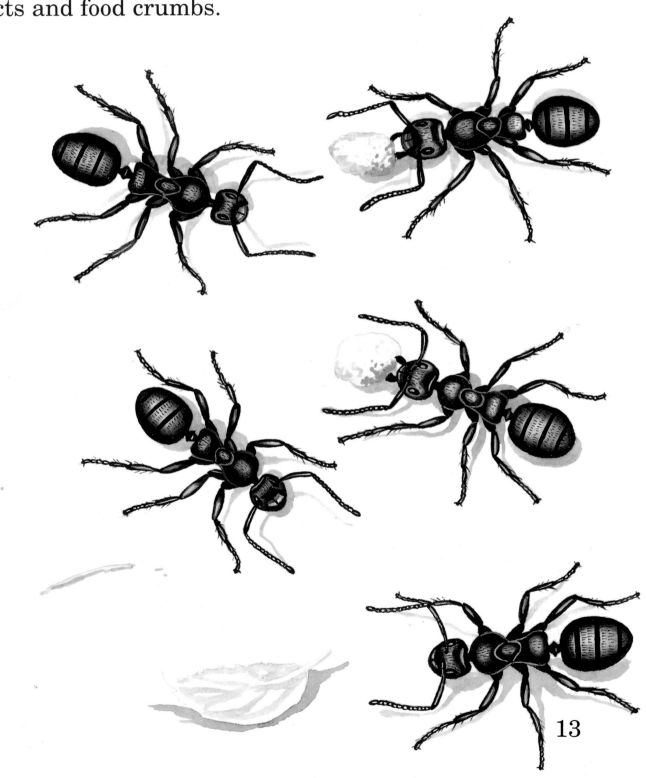

Farming

Worker ants feed the queen with a sugary liquid. Some of this food is nectar which they collect from flowers. They also collect a sugary liquid from greenfly. Greenfly are tiny bugs that feed on a plant's sap.

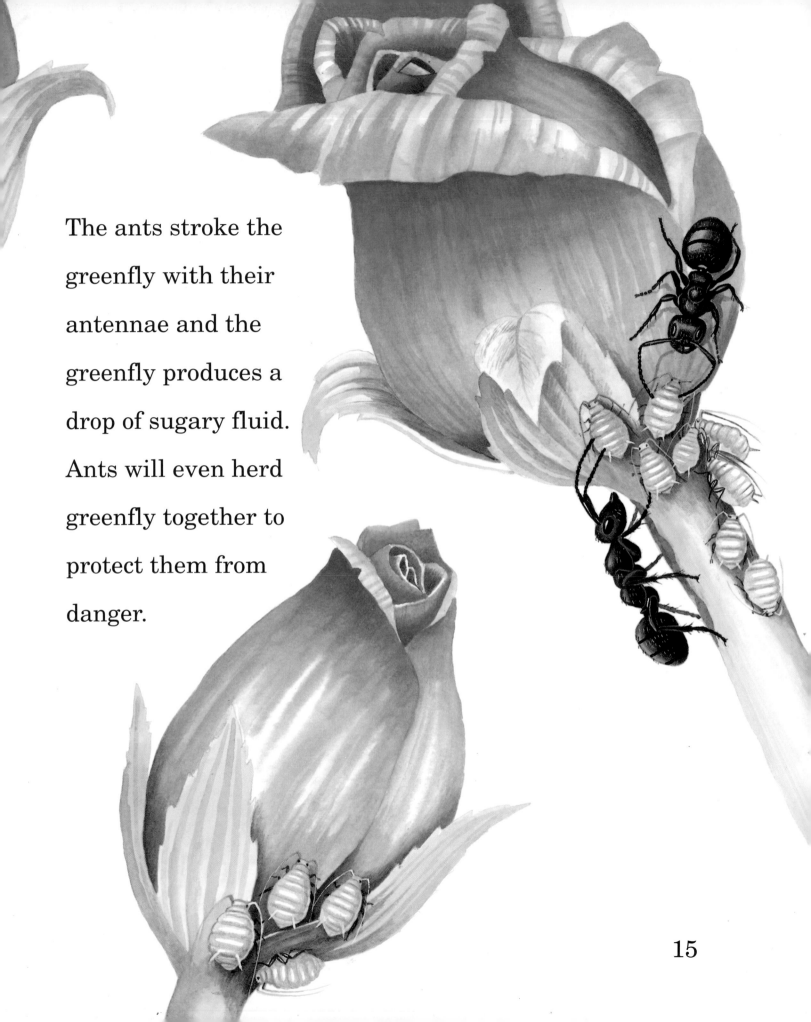

The ants stroke the greenfly with their antennae and the greenfly produces a drop of sugary fluid. Ants will even herd greenfly together to protect them from danger.

15

Ant nest

The ant nest is built by the worker ants. They may build their nest in a field, in a garden or even under the pavement. The nest is made up of lots of tunnels that lead to small chambers.

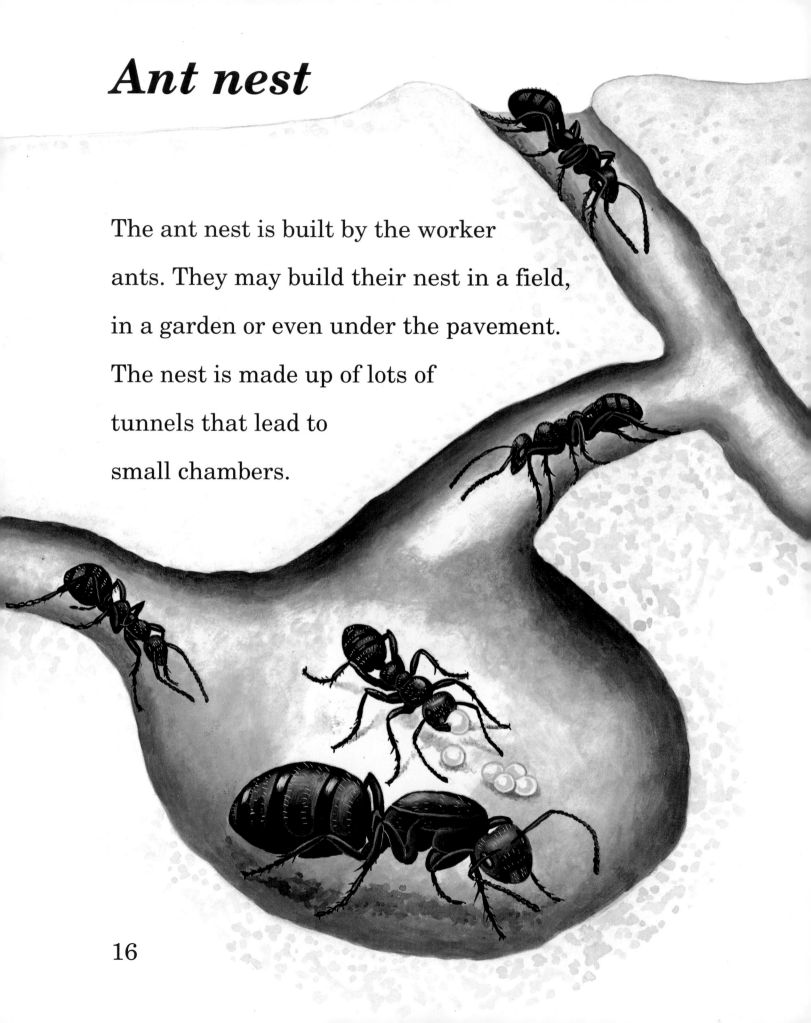

16

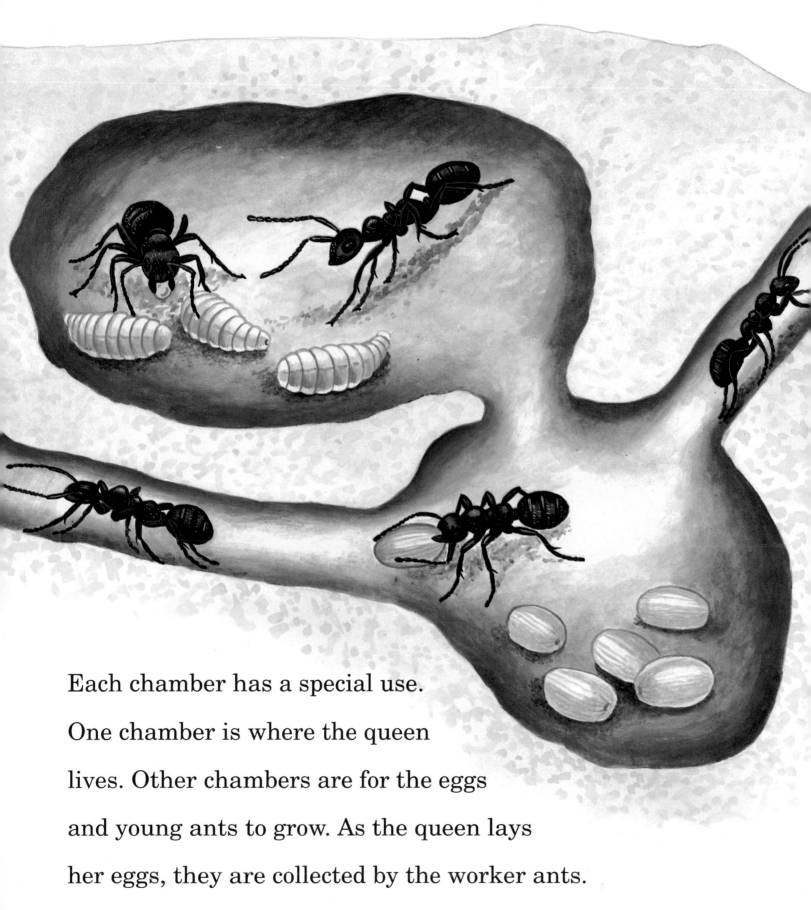

Each chamber has a special use.
One chamber is where the queen
lives. Other chambers are for the eggs
and young ants to grow. As the queen lays
her eggs, they are collected by the worker ants.

Eggs and larvae

The eggs are taken to a special egg hatching chamber. This chamber is near the surface, so that the eggs will be warmed by the sun's heat.

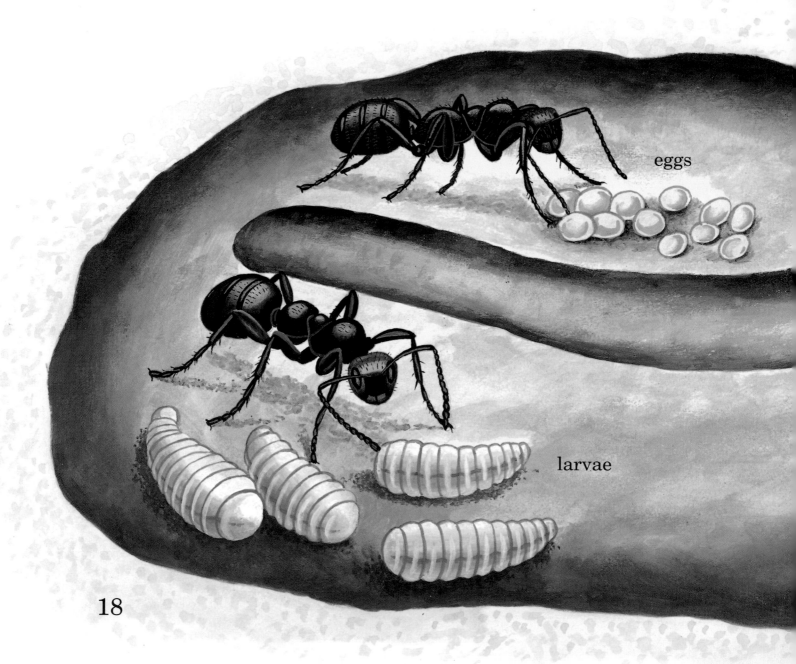

eggs

larvae

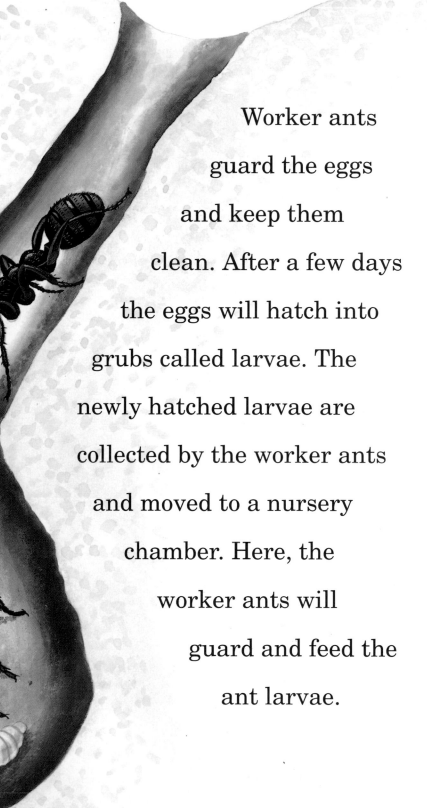

Worker ants guard the eggs and keep them clean. After a few days the eggs will hatch into grubs called larvae. The newly hatched larvae are collected by the worker ants and moved to a nursery chamber. Here, the worker ants will guard and feed the ant larvae.

Cocoon

When the larvae are fully grown they spin a cocoon around themselves. After twenty-one days in their cocoon, the larvae will have become ants. These ants start to break out of their cocoons, with the help of worker ants.

worker ant feeding larva

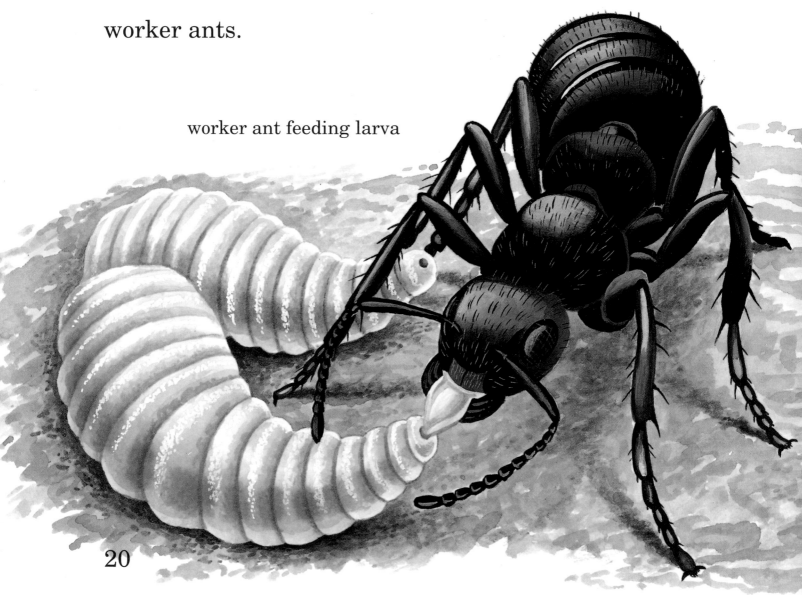

Most of these new ants are also worker ants. In the summer, a few larger cocoons will become new queen ants. At this time, some of the smaller cocoons will become males.

fully grown ant hatching out of cocoon

Dangers

centipede

Ants are often attacked
and eaten by spiders, beetles
and centipedes. They may even
be attacked by other ants. Ants can
protect themselves using their jaws.
They can also squirt a drop of formic acid,
which is like a painful sting.

22

spider

Ants are sometimes eaten by birds and other animals that break into the nest. Ants that nest under a pavement may be accidentally trodden on.

beetle

Repairing the nest

An ant nest may be
accidentally damaged by
a gardener digging the garden.
Worker ants will quickly spread out
around the nest looking for the attacker.
Other worker ants will quickly move any eggs
or cocoons to safety.

When all are safe, the worker ants will quickly repair the damaged nest. Worker ants can carry pieces of soil in their jaws.

Flight

On a warm humid summer day, the new queen ants leave the nest. They fly high up into the sky followed by the males. Many of the flying ants will be eaten by birds but a few will survive and mate.

These queen ants find safe
places to hide during the winter.
The next spring they will lay eggs
and start a new ant colony. The ants in
the old nest get ready for the coming winter.

Other ants

Yellow field ants may also make their nest in your garden. Their dome-shaped nests can sometimes be seen in fields.

28

The wood ant is much larger than the black ant and makes its nest in woodland. Part of the nest is underground; part is above ground in a large mound made of pine needles and twigs.

Life cycle of an ant

1 The female

2 The male

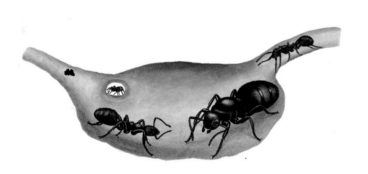

3 The queen

4 Looking for food

5 Farming

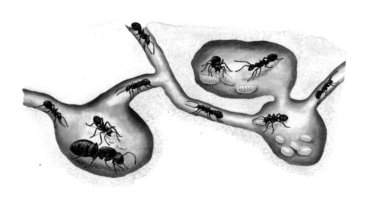

6 Ant nest

7 Eggs and larvae

8 Cocoon

9 Dangers

10 Repairing the nest

11 Flight

Glossary

antennae   Pair of feelers on the head which ants use for touch and smell.

colony   A group of the same type of animal or plant living or growing together.

larva   The ant's feeding and development stage, like the caterpillar of a moth or butterfly.

nectar   A sugary liquid produced by flowers.

queen   A female ant who is able to lay eggs and is the founder of an ant colony.

sap   A solution of mineral salts, sugars etc that circulate in a plant.

worker ant   A female ant that is unable to mate.

Index